Dedication

To my comrades, my family, and those who
carry their own weight in silence.

Unwritten Until Now

The Words I Finally Set Free

Written By: Alma Santiago

Unwritten Until Now: The Words I Finally Set Free
Written and Illustrated by Alma Santiago
Cover by Alma Santiago

Unity House Press
Holyoke, MA
https://unityhouse.press/

ISBN: 979-8-9935714-1-6

Printed in the United States of America
First Edition, 2025

Introduction

Unwritten Until Now: The Words I Finally Set Free

For most of my life, I carried stories I never told. Some were too heavy to speak aloud; others, too sacred to trust to paper. They lived quietly inside me, unfinished, unheard, and unresolved. This book is where they finally found their voice.

"Unwritten Until Now" isn't just a collection of poems, it's a release. It's the moment I stopped editing my truth for the comfort of others. Every page is a step toward healing, forgiveness, and freedom. Some of these words were born from grief and loss; others from love, courage, and resilience. Together, they tell the story of surviving what tried to silence me, and learning that silence is not peace.

Each poem is a piece of me: the soldier, the daughter, the woman, the survivor, and the soul still learning how to be whole. You'll find moments of pain, but also moments of light, because even the hardest stories deserve to end in hope.

If you've ever kept your words locked inside because they felt too heavy, too complicated, or too misunderstood, this book is for you. May it remind you that your voice matters. Your story matters. And even if the world never hears it, the act of writing it down is enough.

This is my truth, finally set free.
 These are the words I could no longer keep unwritten.

Section 1
The Weight I Carry

The Weight I Carry

I learned to bury tears in sand,
with boots laced tight, rifle in hand.
The first salute, I froze, couldn't move,
grief pressed down, nothing to prove.
The cries of others filled the air,
and I stood hollow, lost, aware.

On the radio, voices screamed,
chaos, panic — not a dream.
"Help us now!" — I could not speak,
the silence in me loud, unique.
One survived, the rest were gone,
their echoes haunt me, carry on.

Bombs fell nightly, sky on fire,
I stopped running, I lost desire.
"God, if it's my time, let it be,"
I whispered numb, no will in me.
My husband shot, the news unclear,
I called his mother, choking fear.

So I pulled away, I built my wall,
made no friends, avoided all.
Better to lose no one again,
than risk the pain I held within.
I stopped the news, I stayed inside,
in crowds I shook, with pills I'd hide.

Continued…

The Weight I Carry (continued)

Nyquil nights and sleepless years,
fainting spells, unspoken fears.
Now in boardrooms, work, or flight,
the same old panic grips me tight.
Prepared for loss, for what may come,
I stock my house, I keep my guns.

Cycles of sorrow rise and fall,
I brace myself, I feel it all.
A mother gone, a niece in pain,
old wounds reopen, sharp as flame.
And though I fight, the truth remains,
the weight I carry still has chains.

I could go on, there's more to tell,
but here's enough, you know it well.
The battles linger, though war is past,
its shadows follow, hold me fast.

Buried in Sand, Rifle in Hand

I buried my fear in the desert's heat,
boots sunk deep where the dust and grief meet.
The sun burned down, no mercy, no shade,
a soldier's prayer in silence was made.

Rifle in hand, I became stone,
carving a life in a place not my own.
Every grain carried whispers of war,
of those who would rise, and those no more.

The wind howled truths I tried to ignore,
that survival meant closing a door.
So I buried my sorrow, buried my cries,
beneath the sand where a part of me lies.

But even now, with the desert behind,
I carry the weight in the corners of mind.
Buried in sand, though I came home alive,
a part of my soul never survived.

Shifting Truths

The call came sharp, the message unclear,
"Shot," they said, and froze me with fear.
First an arm, then a hand, then his fault alone
Every word changed the shape of my bones.
I stood suspended, the ground fell away,
Truth rearranged with each phrase they'd say.

I held my breath, clenched fists tight,
Prayed through panic that lasted the night.
War gave me drills, taught me the fight,
But not how to stand when love's struck by fright.
The body survives, but the mind is torn,
Between what's said, and what's still unborn.

In chaos of rumors, my heart was displaced,
Time carved deep lines on my unguarded face.
I learned that survival has many names
Fear, anger, silence, the quiet flames.
And though he lived, the memory stayed,
Of how truth wavered, and strength decayed.

The Arsenal of Quiet Watch

I do not sleep on trust alone,
The world has taught me what's unknown.
So I keep them close, lined in a row,
Silent guardians that few may know.

Each one polished, each one named,
Not for glory, not for fame.
But for the weight of peace at night,
The comfort of knowing I'll stand and fight.

It isn't fear that fuels my hand,
But the need to guard what's mine, my land.
Prepared for storms that never warn,
For dangers quiet, sudden, born.

Some find safety in locks or prayer,
I find mine in steel, in care.
Because the world is sharp, and I've been cut,
So I refuse to stand unarmed, unshut.

Six voices silent, six guards aligned,
Each one steady, each one mine.
Not obsession, not mistrust spun,
But peace in knowing I'm never undone.

Survivor

I've stood in rooms where silence screamed,
where faces blurred into shadows of dreams.
Orders barked, the dust hung still,
I carried a weight nobody should fill.

The blast took many, but I remained,
a living scar, a soul unnamed.
Why them, not me? I'll never know,
the question follows wherever I go.

Nights are crowded though I'm alone,
voices echo in blood and bone.
The medals shine but can't disguise,
the guilt that stares through weary eyes.

I march each day, though the battle is past,
haunted by ghosts that were taken too fast.
No victory here, no glory to claim
just one survivor, whispering names.

Section 2
Margins of Love and War

Margins of Love and War

Between love and duty I carved my name,
on paper stained with fire and flame.
Your letters bled through miles of sand,
while I held a rifle instead of your hand.

I learned to kiss you in broken lines,
to read between silence and military time.
Our love existed in the margins, thin,
where war kept ending what could not begin.

You asked for my heart, I gave you a piece,
but war took the rest and offered no peace.
How do you love when the nights are so far,
when trust is a shadow of who we are?

Still I wrote, though the pages tore,
love in the margins of love and war.
And even now, with the battles behind,
those margins remain etched in my mind.

Storm Inside

I wanted to leave, to run, to hide,
to mend the cracks where the storm resides.
Not broken, but bending, pulled apart,
a battle of silence inside my heart.

I dreamed of returning as someone new,
stronger, lighter, a brighter view.
To stand before you, without the weight,
to offer love that storms can't take.

But here I am, with the thunder near,
lightning flashing in shadows of fear.
I cannot escape what I hold within,
the storm inside is where I begin.

So love me not for the calm I feign,
but for weathering nights of relentless rain.
For I am the storm, and the storm is me,
a truth I carry, and long to set free.

My Voice

In crowded rooms my voice is weak,
the words get tangled when I speak.
My tongue grows heavy, thought takes flight,
but on the page, the words ignite.

A pen can carve what lips can't give,
it shows the way I truly live.
Do not mistake this ink for fear,
each line I write pulls you more near.

I want to speak, to meet your eyes,
but silence wins, my courage dies.
So let me write, let letters show,
the love, the care you need to know.

These written words may be my shield,
but still they open what I've sealed.
And if my voice feels small, withdrawn,
these lines will live when I am gone.

The Things I Couldn't Say

The things I couldn't say lived in my chest,
words unspoken, unrest confessed.
Each glance, each pause, a heavy stone,
a language of silence all my own.

I couldn't tell you the nights I bled,
fighting battles inside my head.
Couldn't explain the way I'd hide,
smiling outside while I crumbled inside.

I wanted to speak, but the words would choke,
like ash and smoke from a fire I stoked.
So I let the silence build its wall,
and hoped you'd hear the unspoken call.

But love can't thrive on things unsaid,
on ghosts of truths that live instead.
Still I carry them, day by day,
all the things I couldn't say.

Section 3
Threads of Unity

Threads of Unity

We are bound by threads too strong to fray,
woven in love that will not decay.
Across the miles, through war and strife,
those threads have carried me through my life.

One thread for mother, steady and true,
the anchor I clung to when skies turned blue.
Threads for my sisters, fierce and kind,
braiding strength into my mind.

And mine, the last, though worn and scarred,
still tied to theirs, still holding hard.
Together we form a word complete,
a circle of love no war can defeat.

Even as years pull us apart,
Unity lives in the fabric of heart.
Threads may stretch, but they never sever
woven in family, bound forever.

Unity Across Oceans

Five letters carved, five hearts aligned,
UNITY, a bond no war could unwind.
A necklace given, each pendant worn,
A promise held when the night felt torn.
Before I left, I swore aloud,
We'd stay together, through smoke and crowd.

In mailrooms crowded with nameless calls,
I scanned the stacks, the endless walls.
And there they were, marked bold, in view,
UNITY scrawled, I already knew.
Care packages glowing with love inside,
A word so small, yet a lifeline wide.

It carried me through the desert's despair,
A whispered truth that someone still cared.
That even when oceans stretched between,
The word was a bridge, a sacred scene.
UNITY became more than a name,
It was survival, it was flame.

Unity Story

Before my first deployment, I searched for a way
to keep my family with me when I was far away.
I found it in five letters, simple, strong,
a word that could carry us all along.

UNITY.

I gave each of them a pendant to wear:
U for my mother, the heart always there.
N, I, and T for my sisters who raised me,
Y for myself, the bond that amazed me.

I told them no matter the miles, the fight,
we would always be together, always in sight.
And when the packages came across the sea,
UNITY scrawled bold, they called out to me.

From across the mailroom, I knew they were mine,
a lifeline of love through the harshest of times.
That word became anchor, armor, prayer,
reminding me always: they were there.

UNITY.

It isn't just letters, it isn't just me.
It's the strength of my family
and the promise we'll always be.

The Sacred Word

UNITY—my vow, my name, my flame,
But when borrowed by others, it's not the same.
I gave my life to keep it whole,
A promise carved deep into my soul.

I have no children, no branch of my own,
This family's my garden, my only home.
Yet when they use it, loose and wide,
It cuts like betrayal I cannot hide.

I promised Mom I'd hold it fast,
That UNITY would always last.
But division grows, and silence reigns,
And I'm left holding broken chains.

Still, I write these words so they'll see
The weight this word still carries in me.

The Night She Left

I sat through every test and scan,
appointments daily, hand in hand.
Not as her child with time to spare,
but as her nurse in every chair.
I measured meds, I watched her fade,
a year and half of roles we played.

I wanted talks, advice, her voice,
but sickness stripped away the choice.
Each morning brought the same old dread
is this the day she won't rise from bed?
The daughter in me lost her place,
to charts and pills and tight embrace.

Then came the call, her breath was gone,
a quiet night, her life withdrawn.
That very day, she'd been moved away,
to hospice halls where she'd always say:
Don't you dare put me there, not me,
her lifelong plea, our family's creed.

And yet one night was all it took,
her story closed, her final book.
I laughed, I cried, I couldn't believe,
how fate had written such a weave.
The place she swore she'd never be,
became the door to eternity.

Continued...

The Night She Left (continued)

I called my sisters, gathered near,
we faced my father, broken with fear.
He saw us standing, knew the sound,
of love now buried in the ground.
Forty years bound in endless grace,
undone in one embrace, erased.

That night remains, etched in my chest,
a bitter joke, a final test.
I longed for her, not as a chart,
but as my mom, her voice, her heart.
And though she's gone, her love is mine,
a thread unbroken, across all time.

Promise to Mom

I swore to keep the bond we knew,
the word of Unity, strong and true.
I begged my sisters, hear me now,
I made to Mom a sacred vow.

The necklaces, the letters worn,
the nights of prayer when we were torn.
Her voice still calls from where she rests,
"Protect each other, give your best."

No other crowd can wear this name;
it's ours alone, it holds our flame.
Yet still I fear the ties grow weak,
we seldom share the words we speak.

I write because my voice won't stay,
when face-to-face, I look away.
But paper holds the truth I send,
to keep us whole until the end.

For Dad, what will we do?
I ask in love, I turn to you.
Together strong, not torn apart,
Unity beats in one great heart.

Birth

A cry broke through, the world stood still,
new life arrived, a sacred thrill.
Her tiny hands, her breathing fast,
a future bright, the past surpassed.

Her skin so soft, her heartbeat near,
her eyes not yet to hold the clear.
But in her face, I saw the line,
the roots of ours, the threads divine.

Another branch upon our tree,
a chance to heal, a chance to be.
Her laughter someday yet to start,
already mends my broken heart.

Her birth a gift, her voice a song,
a reason now to still be strong.
And when the world feels cold, untrue,
I'll think of her, and make it through.

The Weight of Goodbye

Dear Luna, girl, my heart, my friend,
your love was steady, without end.
You came to me when I was torn,
just out of war, bruised, newly worn.

A pup, yet somehow you could see
the broken, hidden parts of me.
No questions asked, you stayed near,
a silent voice that calmed my fear.

Through nights of grief, through days of pain,
you laid beside me in the rain.
No judgment passed, no heavy ask,
just love that met my every task.

Twelve years you gave, soft eyes, warm paws,
a loyal soul with no true flaws.
Your wagging tail, your gentle gaze,
lit up my darkest, longest days.

And in the end, the hardest choice,
I silenced my own breaking voice.
I let you go, though torn apart,
a mercy born from an aching heart.

I still look back, I still expect,
the sound of paws, the love unchecked.
Another dog may fill the space,
but none can take your sacred place.

Continued...

The Weight of Goodbye (continued)

You were my anchor, once, for life,
my healing balm through loss and strife.
A once-in-a-lifetime bond so true,
no soul will ever be like you.

So run now free, no pain, no chain,
with Mom above, in skies of rain.
I'll see you there when the time is due,
until that day, I carry you.

In Loving Memory (Mom)

I count the days though the years move on,
since the light went out, since you were gone.
March winds whispered, April wept,
the weight of goodbye in silence kept.

I held your hand but could not stay,
the clock moved fast, it stole that day.
A daughter's cry could not be heard,
grief took root where love once stirred.

The house feels empty, though voices near,
your absence lingers in every tear.
I search for you in the quiet air,
in the scent of roses, I find you there.

No grave, no stone can hold you down,
you live in my heart, where love is found.
Though April 14 carved its scar,
your memory shines, my guiding star.

For My Father

He worked through years with calloused hands,
through burning sun and shifting sands.
A steady man, both firm and true,
the kind of strength I always knew.

He taught me silence can speak loud,
humble steps, but never proud.
His love was simple, sharp, and clear,
a quiet anchor always near.

The world may change, but he stands fast,
built from stories, built to last.
Forty years bound to Mom's embrace,
now sorrow lingers on his face.

I see the weight he tries to hide,
the grief that pulls him from inside.
Yet still he wakes, yet still he fights,
a man of mornings, not of nights.

For all he gave, I now must be
the guard for him as he was for me.
My father's strength runs in my veins,
his love endures, though time remains.

Section 4
Where Silence Speaks

Where Silence Speaks

The quiet is louder than any sound,
it presses in, it pulls me down.
No battle cry, no marching feet,
just the silence where shadows meet.

I sit with thoughts I cannot name,
guilt and grief, a shapeless flame.
Words unspoken, locked away,
the silence says what I can't say.

It tells of nights I could not sleep,
of wounds too buried, cut too deep.
Of smiles I wore, of masks I made,
of storms inside that never fade.

And though the world sees calm and peace,
within me rages a war's release.
For silence holds what my voice won't keep
my story lives where silence speaks.

Her Silence, My Guilt

She came to me to escape the hate,
Bullies behind her, a chance to create.
A home of safety, or so I dreamed,
But the silence cut deeper than it seemed.
On my birthday, a cry not mine
Her body broken, her soul out of line.

I told myself it was not my fault,
But guilt pressed heavy, a locked-up vault.
I left her alone, I left her to ache,
The same hollow loneliness I couldn't shake.
Now when I sit in these empty rooms,
I wonder if she felt these tombs.

The echo of her pain lives here,
A shadow that whispers year by year.
I know I loved, I know I tried,
But some truths remain where tears have dried.
Her silence carved into my skin,
A reminder of loss, where it begins.

Ache in the Morning

I wake with pain from head to feet,
a body stiff, a heavy beat.
The morning greets with aching hands,
joints on fire, no one understands.

It takes me hours to find my stride,
to move the weight I hold inside.
The pills bring comfort, but not for long,
the ache remains, a quiet song.

By night it returns, the cycle repeats,
a war within that no one sees.
No battlefield, no medals shown,
just silent wounds I bear alone.

I smile, I stand, I play my part,
but the ache still whispers inside my heart.
A soldier's fight without the fame
each morning begins the same.

11:25 P.M.

The clock ticks heavy, past eleven at night,
I should be resting, but nothing feels right.
My body exhausted, my spirit awake,
A hollow emptiness I cannot shake.

I wander inside myself, lost and bare,
Searching for something that isn't there.
Why now, why this hour, why this pain?
The silence roars, a familiar chain.

The bed becomes a battlefield plain,
Pillows soaked in restless rain.
No answer comes, just aching air,
And I wonder if hope still waits somewhere.

Fear of Being Alone

The room is loud with echoes near,
yet no one answers, none can hear.
The quiet cuts, the shadows stay,
I pace the night, I hide by day.

The bed feels vast, the covers cold,
my chest is tight, my hands won't hold.
Each creak, each sigh, each fleeting sound,
reminds me no one else is found.

But in the mirror, I'm not gone,
the strength inside keeps holding on.
Alone, perhaps, but not undone,
I face the dark until there's sun.

If loneliness is what I bear,
I'll teach myself that I still care.
And when the morning breaks the night,
I'll rise again, I'll seek the light.

The Girl I Lost

There was a time waterfalls knew my name,
Adventures sparked without fear or shame.
I was the girl who roamed alone,
Confident, fearless, the world my own.

Clubs, strangers, laughter, light,
I danced through day, I conquered night.
Every road a story, every stop a flame,
Now I mourn the girl who is not the same.

She faded fast, replaced by fear,
Her bold voice silenced year by year.
I scroll through photos, the proof still there,
Of a spirit that lived without despair.

And though she's gone, she still survives,
In whispers, in memories, in sparks that thrive.
I'll find her again, when sorrow's done
That fearless girl, I was once the one.

Section 5
The Echo of Unity

Carried Home in Poems

I could not bring them home in hand,
the years I lost, the miles of sand.
The faces gone, the nights I wept,
the secrets heavy, the silence kept.

But words can travel where bodies can't,
they breathe the truth my voice recants.
They carry the weight I could not bear,
and lay it down for others to share.

Each line a bridge, each verse a key,
unlocking the grief inside of me.
And though the battles are mine alone,
my story is carried, my heart is shown.

So if you wonder where I've been,
look in the pages where I begin.
What I could not hold, I've set in stone
a life, a love, now carried home.

The Echo of Unity

A word once worn around our necks,
five letters strong, five lives it protects.
Through deserts, storms, and oceans wide,
UNITY carried us side by side.

It echoed in care from across the sea,
boxes marked bold so I'd know they were for me.
It echoed in voices when distance grew long,
reminding my spirit where I belong.

And even as years take loved ones away,
the echo of Unity still guides my way.
It whispers of bonds no time can sever,
of love that endures, unbroken, forever.

Not just a word, not just a chain,
but a promise that lives through joy and pain.
The echo resounds, it will always be
my family, my anchor, my Unity.

Solo Trip

The cliffs of green, the ocean wild,
a land that called me, fierce yet mild.
The rain fell soft, the wind blew near,
I faced the world without my fear.

The cobbled streets, the voices loud,
I walked alone but felt a crowd.
No chain of past, no weight of war,
just open sky, an endless shore.

A pint was raised, a toast alone,
yet in that moment I was home.
The girl I lost returned to me,
her spirit strong, her soul set free.

I learned that solitude can sing,
a hymn of flight, a prayer on wing.
Ireland's breath, the sea's refrain,
gave me myself, alive again.

Future Road

The open road, the wheels will spin,
a map of dreams I'll wander in.
With books to share, with tales to tell,
small towns will know me all too well.

I'll park beneath the evening skies,
read stories where the silence lies.
Children gather, voices bright,
their laughter heals the darkest night.

The engine hums, the miles unfold,
I trade my burdens, chase the bold.
Each chapter read, each smile I see,
reminds me who I'm meant to be.

The road ahead may twist and wind,
but peace is what I hope to find.
Through every stop, through dusk and dawn,
the journey heals, the road goes on.

Unwritten Until Now

For years, I carried words inside,
buried in silence, nowhere to hide.
They lived in shadows, they burned my chest,
letters unsent, confessions suppressed.

I spoke through actions, through weary eyes,
through broken sleep and quiet sighs.
But the truth remained, a stubborn vow,
unwritten then, but written now.

These pages hold the weight I bore,
the love, the loss, the endless war.
Not polished, perfect, or free of scars,
but pieces of me, just as they are.

So if you read them, read them true
these words were carried to give to you.
They are my past, my voice, my vow,
unwritten until now.

www.ingramcontent.com/pod-product-compliance
Lightning Source LLC
Chambersburg PA
CBHW020812130626
46554CB00006B/2391